ENDORSEMENTS

Terri Levine's book, *About To Break,* is one of the best I have read on the topic of forgiveness and being your authentic self. She shares her story in a way that it is almost impossible not to gain permission to be your authentic self and forgive those in your life that may have hurt you in a way that allows you to move forward. It is rare to find someone like Terri who is so successful and willing to be vulnerable at such a deep level to help others. This book is a must read for everyone who wants more in their life or has been blocked by past events. It is well written and touched me at a soul level. This book has the ability to allow you to change your life on a way that no other can. It did for me. Thank you Terri for being vulnerable and authentic. You are pure love.

Rhonda Sher
LinkedIn Consultant
RhondaLSher.com

I've known Terri Levine and read many of her business books and was curious about what she would reveal in her autobiography. I didn't expect to receive a lesson so valuable on forgiveness which is so healthy and valuable for every human being.

In this well-written book, *About To Break,* Terri shares her life story and teaches how to set yourself free. This wonderful book will truly enable you to be an agent of healing and love. Don't wait. Grab a copy for yourself and anyone you have wronged.

Ben Gay III
The Closers
WWW.BFG3.COM

WOW! Can I relate to your new book, *About To Break,* Terri! After more than 21 years of emotional, mental, and physical abuse, working with some of the top elite therapists, coaches & mentors in the world, earning multiple certifications, learning to let go, love and forgive myself, have realized you have a gift shift. We can never stop moving and learning from our higher power and you have given us so many amazing tools, exercises, and gifts here, for transformation and expansion. Thank you for being so authentic, transparent and opening yourself up to the world to heal others. This book will change lives, as it already has mine, again on a much deeper level. This is a must read, for forgiveness and self-love... beautiful you! I love you Terri Levine.

-Crystal Davis
#1 International Best Selling Author of
"The Authentic Driven Life"
303-848-2919
Crystal@CrystalODavis.com

About to Break has the secret sauce to life and business. I know Terri Levine, her stories, her tools and her self forgiveness shone through me whilst I read her book.

I now really know Terri Levine and I know more of myself.

I trust you grow from this book as much as I did.

Di Downie
International Best Seller of A High Heels Paradox
https://www.didownie.com

If you want to live your life free from the burdens of anger, frustration, guilt and sadness, look no further than Terri Levine's latest book, *About To Break*.

- John J. Fenton, best selling author of
5 Minute Mastery™, The Surprising Secrets
for Transforming Your Stress to Success
and Mastering What's Important

The Author, Terri Levine, in her book *About To Break* gives an honest, vulnerable depiction of real life situations and her journey to heal from the past pain and anger. Her in depth step by step process leads a person to hope again and allows healing to take place for more peace and love.

Jodi Harman
Founder, Marriage Makeover
Author of The Girlfriend Effect
www.jodiharman.com

Two top alternative healing doctors I know say they've never encountered a case of cancer without a root of unforgiveness. Together they have worked with thousands. This insightful revelation alone is reason enough to read Terri Levine's book *About to Break*. I wholeheartedly endorse her message and her healing process because it has worked for me. Enjoy her captivating stories and apply these simple strategies to your life. Freedom awaits.

Patrice Lynn, Amazon #1 Best-selling Author of
RISE to Success, and The Brain Training Expert.
www.PatriceLynn.com

ABOUT TO BREAK

THE PATH TO TRUE FORGIVENESS

TERRI LEVINE

Published by Authors Place Press
9885 Wyecliff Drive, Suite 200
Highlands Ranch, CO 80126
AuthorsPlace.com

Manufactured in the United States of America.

ISBN: 978-1-62865-662-6

OTHER TITLES BY THIS AUTHOR

*Turbocharge: How to Transform Your Business
as a Heart-repreneur*

Turbocharge Your Business

Elite Business Systems

The Innovators

The Ultimate Game Plan

Contents

Foreword

by Sheila Pearl

There is no love without forgiveness, and there is no forgiveness without love.
– Bryant H. McGill

WHY IS IT THAT MOST WORLD religions teach about the value of forgiveness? It seems to be fundamental to the human condition to have the need to forgive, doesn't it? And yet...for each of us, it remains a challenge of one magnitude or another to bring ourselves to forgive another for wrongs, insults, and abuses we've experienced. No matter how we slice this loaf of bread, forgiveness is necessary, yet it is for most of us humans difficult at best to achieve mastery with this assignment.

In the work I've been doing as psychotherapist and relationship coach for over three decades, I have witnessed the ability to forgive to be the most challenging frontier. Yet, everyone wants "joy", "happiness" and "love" in their lives. As McGill wisely says: There is no love without forgiveness, and there is no forgiveness without love. In order for each of us to experience the joy and satisfaction of love in our lives, we are each required to first engage in the practice of self-love which presumes forgiveness of the self for real or perceived wrongs, insults or abuses against the self. Once we have mastered self-love, we are then in a position to love others – and that requires that we then engage in the practice of forgiveness of others for all the ways in which they have wronged, insulted and/or abused us.

In the word forgiveness is the word give. Key to the magic of loving relationships with ourselves and others is the act of giving. Yet, without receiving the act of giving is empty. Hence, we humans are designed to give and to receive. The giver cannot experience giving unless there is a receiver. Obviously, the receiver stands with empty hands when there is no giver. And so it goes, the essential cycle of giving and receiving: each needing the other in order to exist. Without giving and receiving, there is no love, since love is the creative energy of the universe and all that we are. There must be a constant flow of giving and receiving for all creativity to exist. When we hold anger, blame, judgment, grudges and resentment, we stop the flow of open-hearted giving and receiving. We withhold, we feel stuck, we are mired in fear and the dark energies that constrict life and joy.

When we keep our hearts open to love, when we remain open to being both the giver and the receiver, we are holding the space for joy, for happiness, for satisfaction, and most important, for loving engagement with our lives. The greatest obstacle to this open-hearted posture of loving engagement with life itself is the inability to forgive ourselves and others. To the extent that we feel stuck in our own fears, anger and resentment, we prevent ourselves from experiencing the fulness of life.

The teachings of forgiveness have been repeated for thousands of years, handed down from one generation to the next: yet, we need the teachings to be transmitted constantly, in many different ways, over and over again. The repetition of the message, the telling of the stories, the vast variety of ways in which the lesson is taught is essential for each generation. We will most likely never evolve to the level of supreme awareness in which the teaching of this fundamental lesson will cease to be relevant. We crave new storytellers; our hearts and minds are hungry for innovative tools and guidance for how we can best achieve our own love of self and our ability to forgive ourselves and others.

Terri Levine's new book has come to us at just the right time, and her stories are told with a level of raw authenticity and imagination that go straight to the heart. Terri's brilliance for reducing the most complicated subject to its simple elegant essence is alive on each page of this important book.

If you are among that growing number of human beings who are longing for spiritual and emotional liberation from the poison of holding grudges against others, of blaming others for your pain, of judging yourself for perceived sins...this book is for you! This little gem contains stories that illustrate time-tested wisdom and techniques that offer easy-to-follow steps to accomplish forgiveness.

This is a book which has been written for you to read often – the more you read it, the more you remind yourself of the steps to forgiveness, the more you will bring Terri's important message into your heart.

Sheila Pearl, M.S.W.

Certified Life Coach and Spiritual Teacher

Bestselling Amazon Author of "Ageless & Sexy: The Magic of Big Love—Getting Comfortable with Uncertainty"

PREFACE

HUMAN BEINGS, BEING HUMAN, have a problem with forgiveness. Why? Because our minds dwell in the past and not in the current moment. We keep bringing up past experiences and feelings and staying in our anger, disgust, sadness, and disappointment — consciously or unconsciously.

This book will allow you to actually forgive yourself and others and to be free of the burden of anger, frustration, disappointment, and sadness — with circumstances, with yourself, and with others. The processes here actually work and will transform your life from the inside out.

You didn't learn forgiveness because no one bothered to teach it to you. It's not your fault. I am going to share the solution and show you exactly the steps that will have you become a forgiving and loving person with ease.

You will find yourself releasing guilt and allowing in more love and compassion, which will result in your life being even more delicious.

I stood in your shoes. I was angry, sad, and upset, and I held a grudge against people, experiences, and even myself. I learned to be a forgiving and loving person who developed a process that worked for me and for my client family members as well.

INTRODUCTION

THIS BOOK CAME TO FRUITION after I found a way of forgiving myself, my life experiences, and people in my life. I shared pieces of this on Facebook Live, Facebook posts, and with my client family members. Pretty soon people were asking me to write this book.

I usually don't write books on personal coaching or personal issues, even though I am trained as a clinical psychologist and a master life coach. I do business consulting and tend not to work with clients on anything else.

However, I felt I was called to write this book, as the process of my life-coaching was helping so many people. I felt I could not keep this information from others, as I knew it could turn out to be immensely helpful to many people.

You are going to find three amazing processes in this book. Each one by itself is very powerful and will work for you. When you combine them, it will allow you to fully and deeply *release* your perceived hurts and the subsequent resentments they bring. You will become a person who forgives — not forgive and forget — with love and understanding. You will also fall in love with yourself and treat yourself with kindness and compassion from this point forward.

I got to a point in my life where I was not loving at all — neither to others nor to myself. I felt sad and confused, and I wanted to run from my life. I had no understanding of what was happening to me.

On my journey, I found a person who showed me unconditional love and forgiveness at the deepest level. When you read what happened, you will probably not expect this person to forgive me. Trust me: I tell all.

This book is transparently autobiographical. As you read these chapters, you will walk with me into my childhood memories and discover events and people whom I had not forgiven in my more than six decades on the planet.

I know you will see some of yourself in me. It's *your* time right this minute to have a more incredible life. When you learn to forgive yourself and others, you will see that this has been the missing element — the one that has prevented you from you getting the maximum juice from your life. Don't wait one second longer to have the most incredible life experience ever. Dive into this book *fully* — right now.

Make sure you do each of the three exercises in full. When you've finished reading this book, you will know that magic has happened. Let me share two quick stories with you, so you know exactly what to expect.

The first story is from a client family member with whom I shared the process as I was writing this book. My client had not spoken with her father for more than forty years because of the physical, sexual, and emotional abuse she had endured from him. She found herself able to fully let go of the years of anger, sadness, guilt, and Post Traumatic Stress Disorder (PTSD). Even though she had spent years in treatment with psychologists and counselors, had taken self-help courses and seminars, and had hired many life coaches, she had not forgiven her father or herself. She told me that, after she did the exercises in this book, she found herself *free*.

> *I can't believe it! For the first time in my entire life, I have not a speck of anger towards my father. I have no need to speak with him or to see him, yet I have love in my heart for him and know he was doing the best he could with his life's circumstances. I actually sent him love and light and meant it. I also no longer believe I have PTSD and instead accept that I am health, whole and perfect as I am, and I choose love all the time. I love myself and all those around me and have gratitude for all my life experiences. Let me tell you, my friends: my family*

and my therapists and coaches almost can't believe it, and everyone tells me I look ten years younger and that if I keep smiling so big, I will crack my face!

The other story is from an acquaintance I took through the processes you are about to journey on with me at your side.

I was so angry, and every day I felt more and more anger. I actually felt I could harm this person who had wronged me financially. I decided to try your exercises but didn't believe they were going to make any difference. Then, just two days ago, I encountered the woman I had been referring to as "the witch." I smiled at her unconsciously. I caught myself doing it and was shocked. Then, I checked inside myself and found I had no anger toward her. I don't understand it, yet I really like this new way of being. I also notice I am becoming gentler and kinder with myself and am more accepting of each person I meet. I walk down the street smiling at everyone from a genuine place of love and acceptance. Wow! This book is going to be a game-changer, and I will buy a copy for each person I had a grudge against — and for all my coworkers, family, and friends, too.

Get ready! Now it's your turn to break through. When you do, I want to hear your stories. Write your review on Amazon, so I can read your story. Get copies of this book for your friends, those you need to make amends with, and all those you love.

Don't wait another second, as these pages will reveal a process that will improve your health, well-being, self-confidence, ability to love, ability to make money, and your ability to create relationships beyond your wildest expectations.

DEDICATION

My dearest Sarah,

I wrote this book thinking of you. I admire and respect you for your maturity, your unconditional love, and your ability to forgive. I will love you always and all ways, with the ultimate affection and appreciation for you.

Your Aunt T

MY JOURNEY

I love you.

I'm sorry.

Please forgive me.

Thank you.

Dr. Len and Dr. Joe Vitale

DEAR READER,

As I sat down to begin writing this book, I found myself uncertain where and how to begin sharing my journey with you. I was confused. I wondered if I should I begin at the point, a few years ago, when I actually learned what forgiveness really meant. Or should I begin when I was a young girl and almost burned alive? Or by telling you about the beatings I suffered in my life? Or should I begin at a different point, when I was sexually harassed?

I began writing this book sixteen times, and each time I found myself very confused about where I should begin. Then I recalled the words of the late Stephen Covey, "Begin with the end in mind." So, that is exactly what I am going to do. I am going to share transparently, leaving nothing out, and tell you what has occurred in my life that has opened my eyes and heart to really, truly, and deeply understand forgiveness. Throughout this book, I will share actual stories of my journey to allow you to open new pathways of forgiveness and to learn how to truly let go.

Although you might not relate to all of my stories, situations, and experiences, I know you will relate to some. I want you to let in this information so that you can transform your life by being a person who truly forgives on *every* level. I don't mean "forgive and forget." I mean forgive with love in your heart, no matter what has happened. You may be thinking,

"No matter what?" You may be saying, "Terri, you don't know me … you don't know what's happened to me, and you don't know about the circumstances and people that I cannot forgive!"

I certainly don't know your situation. What I do know is that I have been dealt a lot of cards that would cause many people to not forgive a person, a group of people, or an experience. The change that forgiveness made in all aspects of my life has shaped me into the person that I am in this moment — a person who is more self-loving, is compassionate towards others, and has a much bigger heart than I ever thought possible.

As you read this book, I ask you to open your heart, imagine yourself truly forgiving, and not worry about what will happen if you forgive. I know from sharing this information with my client family members that what I am going to reveal to you will truly change you from the inside. I know that people feel they are actually *about to break*, like I once felt. When they find a way to forgive people, situations, their own life circumstances, and — most importantly —

themselves, they will create a new kind of happiness that they've never experienced. I don't care how bad life may seem or how much you may want to pack up and run away from the past. I can only tell you that, when you make the change that I made, your life will truly change.

I want you to know that I don't toss off words such as "transformation" or "your life will change" lightly. I say these words because they are the truth.

As odd as it may sound, while I am writing this, I can tell you with absolute, one-hundred-percent certainty that I am not sorry any of those circumstances happened. I actually accept that each person and each experience is a lesson, a gift and a blessing in my life. I'm not sorry about the people who entered my life, the things that they did or said, the experiences I had with them, or the circumstances that have come to be. I'm even not sorry about my own behaviors.

Here is what I know: I am here on this planet going through what I am going through in each moment, and I can make use of what is occurring and learn from these moments. If I believe that everything that happens in my life helps me grow to live more fully, helps me be more loving, helps me accept more love, and allows me to help others, then forgiveness is a necessity.

You are on your own journey. At times your journey may not look too exciting, may not be a lot of fun, and may seem very difficult. It's just the way you are experiencing life *in this moment*. I am going to help you understand who you are and learn how to forgive without guilt but with love for yourself and for others. There is nothing more beautiful than fully forgiving.

I am on a journey, just like you — learning every single day. I don't know what I don't know. If you knew it all, or if I knew it all, there would be nothing to share and nothing to learn.

After you finish reading this book, I request you share some of your own stories. We are in this together. We can laugh at ourselves, laugh at others, and use our humor to allow us to see ourselves and our lives as less self-important than they really are.

I am sorry if I have stepped on your toes or offended you during this chapter. I am called to deeply impact your life and serve you through this book. My experience as a clinical psychologist and as a life coach taught me to speak my truth.

I want you to mark this book up with hints, with tips, circling solutions that might help you. Jump in with me, and allow me to be your coach and your guide as I share my own story. I was literally feeling that I was *about to break*, but I came through that and woke up to this sweet life that opened my heart up to an entire spectrum of love that truly surrounds me each and every moment.

I thank you for buying this book, because my goal is to touch hundreds of thousands of people and to create momentum for forgiveness. Please inform others of this book and encourage them to get their own copies. Buy some as gifts for those you love, so that others on their journey can be part of the healing that happens when we become more forgiving people.

MEMORIES

Mem'ries,
Light the corners of my mind
Misty water-colored memories
Of the way we were
Scattered pictures,
Of the smiles we left behind
Smiles we gave to one another
For the way we were
Can it be that it was all so simple then?
Or has time re-written every line?
If we had the chance to do it all again
Tell me, would we? Could we?
Mem'ries, may be beautiful and yet
What's too painful to remember
We simply choose to forget

So it's the laughter
We will remember
Whenever we remember...
The way we were...
The way we were...

"The Way We Were" — Barbra Streisand

IT WAS A SUNNY DAY in the middle of summer, and six of us kids decided it would be fun to walk across the street, where they were building the new school that we would enter in September. I can remember our excitement about the new, beautiful building where we would embark on our educational journey.

We had all attended kindergarten at PS 16, which was a very old school that had to be closed down due to asbestos. We strolled across the street and wandered around a great big playground that surrounded the school. Although the equipment wasn't in yet, it was really exciting to imagine this playground filled with children and brand-new equipment for us to enjoy. One of the boys, Michael, noticed a huge box that had been left by the construction crew that looked perfect for us to build a tent in. We huddled in the tent, and we were laughing, being silly, and having a wonderful time using our imaginations, pretending we were camping out in the wilderness.

Suddenly, we heard some children's voices and realized that some other children had entered the playground. We imagined they were bears in our campground and decided that, if we were silent in our tent, the bears would run back into the woods. Suddenly, a roaring voice yelled out, "Let's kill the Jews!" In seconds, our cardboard box was in flames. My heart started pounding, and my little legs could barely get out of the box. I struggled and thought I was trapped. I remember seeing the rest of the children, who were a little bit bigger than me, escape from the flaming box. I panicked, but somehow my struggle, my fear, and my desire to survive kicked in, and I was free of the flaming box. I smelled the burning box and heard the boys laughing. I felt afraid and confused, and I was choking from the smoke that had already gotten into my lungs.

My friends and I all began running toward our apartments as fast as we possibly could. Although I was small, I was a pretty quick runner and was glad of that. I remember wanting to look back to see if those boys were chasing us, but fear overcame me, and I continued to run.

When I reached our apartment, I ran up the steps, taking two at a time with my short legs, burst through the door, and instantly started hysterically crying. My mom came running to me and thought perhaps I had fallen or was injured. Through my tears, I explained to her that we had gone across the street to play. I thought she would be angry since we'd been told not to cross that street alone and also to keep away from the construction. I told her that we were playing in a box, we'd heard voices say, "Let's kill the Jews!" and the next thing we knew the box was on fire. I described how I struggled to get out of the box and how we ran back to the apartment complex. My mother held me and comforted me in her arms. I felt safe. I also felt confused.

Why would anyone want to hurt us? We were children playing in a box. Why would people care what religion we happened to be? I had a lot of questions and no answers. My mother did not explain the background of the situation to me and only stroked my hair and told me it was okay and that I was safe — and that we shouldn't have crossed the street and should never play in a construction area.

I began to think that the box had been set on fire because we weren't supposed to be playing there. Yet I was still confused. Those boys didn't set the box on fire because we were playing in the construction area. They did it because we were Jewish.

Later that night, when my father came home, we all discussed what had happened during the day. My father began to talk to me about something called "anti-Semitism." I'd never heard this word before, and I didn't really understand it. Then my mother began to share stories of what had happened in her life as a young child when she'd experienced a lot of hatred just because she was Jewish. My father related similar stories. I had never heard any of these stories before. I also recall having a feeling in my body that I don't believe I'd ever had before. I was still shaking but no longer from fear. The shaking came from something I called "anger," and I wanted to enact revenge on those boys. As a young girl, I couldn't understand how any human being could want to hurt another human being.

For the remainder of the summer, I was no longer excited about going to school. I actually dreaded going to that school, and I wasn't sure what was going to happen at school. Were those boys going to be at the school? Would I be safe if I was playing outside on the playground?

Each day I experienced more and more anger about what had happened with those boys. I kept wanting to lash out at the boys in some way and hurt them, but I knew it wasn't realistic, as I was a pipsqueak of a child.

We all carry so many memories from our childhoods. It's hard to recall the very first memory I had where I felt that I could not forgive someone or forget a circumstance that happened to me. Yet every time I sat down to write this book the same memory came back to me.

Feeling this angry was a bit scary for me. This was the first time in my life that I felt scared and angry at the same time. That entire summer, I remember constantly feeling confused but not expressing my feelings to my parents because I felt this was something private that I was not supposed to talk about.

As life would have it, many years later, someone would enter my life and make comments to me that were also very anti-Semitic. When I heard those comments, I instantly recalled the playground and the cardboard box. The pain of that memory and the emotion that comes with that pain came flooding back to me. Every experience that causes pain leaves us with great emotion. These emotions lie deep within us, and if we are open and curious and willing to look at them, they can be our biggest lessons. When I decided to open my mind and my heart to truly look at my past experiences and the emotional pain they caused, I was able to understand the gifts that each lesson had for me.

I began to question why such terrible things occur. The only conclusion that I've been able to come to is that the experiences and the people I've encountered are there to teach me some kind of a lesson. I pondered. And I pondered. And I pondered.

Then, a few years ago I had an experience that was so frightening that I actually thought it would break me. I thought I would never come back from it. However, the experience became another gift that would change my life forever. Now I realize that everyone I meet is put on the path to meet me because of some connection that we're supposed to have. I keep my mind and my heart open to discover what other lessons I'm supposed to learn.

Today, I believe that everyone I meet and the experiences I have are there for a reason and that every human being is connected to us through our DNA. Many events unfold that I just can't understand. And then, pretty soon, there is some synchronicity about the event or the person who was involved. When I keep my heart open and believe that the Divine has guided people or experiences to me, then I no longer run from them in fear or hold anger or resentment about them.

The biggest fear I had on the day of the box fire was that, when I told my mom I had crossed the street and played at the construction site, I was going to get in trouble. "Trouble" meant that I was going to experience "Mr. Belt."

I can vividly recall the time that I came home from school and April, the older girl in our apartment building, asked if I wanted to go to the playground with her. I was excited to go with April. She was like a sister to me, and the fact that she wanted to spend time with me made me feel really good. I had only one sister, Lynn, who was seven years older than me and really didn't want anything to do with me, because she felt that I was an interference, getting in the way of her friends. Yet April had an interest in me. How exciting!

April and I played on the playground. I remember running, laughing, jumping, going on the seesaw with her, swinging really high and going on the slide over and over again. I was having so much fun and laughing so hard that I didn't want the day to end. Soon it started to get dark, and April said we were late and that we needed to run home. As we entered our apartment complex, she darted off to her apartment below us, and I went running up the steps — only to see a police officer standing in my wide-open front door with my mother. As I came up the steps, the police officer asked my mother, "Is this your child?" My mother immediately grabbed me by the hair, pulled me into the apartment, and smacked me across the face so hard that I fell down. As I lay on the ground, I looked up to see that she had hit me with her shoe that had a three-inch spiked heel on it.

Today if someone did this to their child in front of a police officer, surely, they'd be arrested for child abuse! But back then, the police officer calmly told my mother that he could tell she was happy to see me, had overreacted, and that she probably shouldn't do that again. The pain across my cheek burned. I felt that I deserved to be hit like this since I had done something really bad: April and I lost track of time, and I came home late. I started to feel really bad for my mother, who must have been so worried that she even called the police. She seemed somewhat hysterical, and I went off to my room, sobbing.

I realized my mother was so stressed out thinking that her child had disappeared, and I accepted that she'd just let off some steam — even if it was on my face with a shoe.

As a child, I recall my dad hitting me with "Mr. Belt," mostly on my feet, and I also recall my mom throwing many objects at me — not just a shoe. I really didn't think that I was angry about any of this until I resurfaced the memories, and they started to replay over and over again. One thing I do know is that my parents were doing the very best they could, and I know they certainly loved me and that they did not intend to harm or hurt me. I didn't come with a parenting manual. The seven-year difference between myself and my sister meant that my parents were not young when I was born, and clearly, they had no patience.

Going back to my childhood, another memory surfaces. I was very underweight as a child. I didn't like to eat, and I didn't really have an interest in food. That made my mother very concerned. Every single day, I would dread dinnertime. I would sit at the table just watching while everyone else ate their food. I had no desire to eat. I had to sit at the table every night until bedtime because I had not eaten my dinner.

Meanwhile, my family would leave the table, and I could hear my parents and my sister watching TV after dinner. The tiny apartment allowed me to hear the TV and their laughter, but I was sitting at the table and could not see it or be a part of the family TV time.

I am not certain why I didn't eat with my family when I was a child. Maybe I didn't like my mother's food or maybe there was something else going on that I am not aware of. When I was invited to eat at a friend's home, I ate a lot of food. When I began first grade and started having lunch at school, I ate everything in sight there as well. So, I went from a very thin and frail child to a pudgy girl who later developed some serious weight issues.

It's kind of funny now as I reflect on this, because whenever I gained any weight, my mother gave me a really hard time. This was something I realized that I had not forgiven.

So how do you forgive your dead parents? How do you forgive boys who intended to cause harm or death to other human beings?

I will share the steps as I take you much deeper — into things that are a bit darker and into situations that might seem harder to forgive.

Are you ready to go deeper with me?

How are you feeling as you are reading my words and hearing my stories?

Just notice. Smiling Faces Sometimes

Smiling faces sometimes pretend to be your friend
Smiling faces show no traces of the evil that lurks
within
Smiling faces, smiling faces sometimes
They don't tell the truth
"Smiling Faces Sometimes" — Undisputed
Truth

M Y CHILDHOOD TRANSITIONED into college and into my working career, and I experienced a lot of love and massive business success. I was happily married to my high school sweetheart, and we had time to travel, be with family and friends, and for our hobbies, community, and our spiritual practices. My business was exploding, and I had become somewhat of a celebrity in my industry, with bestselling books, keynote speeches around the world, thousands of client family members who I was helping, and a very successful coach-training school.

Then, I got the phone call.

A woman who'd heard of my success phoned me one day, and I answered the phone. That was odd in itself, as most of my calls were screened by my team members. I thought, at the time, it was a great coincidence. Later, I regretted picking up the phone.

The voice at the other end said, "I was told to connect with you, as we have a lot in common." I was intrigued. We ended up chatting for a long time; I found her very spiritual and flakey, yet I enjoyed the conversation. We eventually decided that we were going to do a joint venture together, as she was a life coach and spirit coach; I was a business and marketing coach, and we both happened to own coach-training schools.

The joint venture went well in terms of finances, although I did find myself producing the bulk of the work, as I have the marketing and sales knowledge that this program ended up really utilizing. We had fun doing the work together, and I got to know her on a personal level.

She said a few things that seemed a bit "off" to me. She told me that, although she was married, she and her husband, every year on their anniversary, evaluate whether or not they want to stay married. To me, that was a bit flakey, and I began to wonder if she had commitment issues.

But that wasn't any of my business, so I just let it go. She also told me that she had a former business partner that she'd ended up suing, but she would not tell me the reason. I found that odd; however, I ignored that signal.

I made it clear to her that she was not my business partner and that our business arrangement was, legally, a joint venture. She agreed completely.

Eventually the joint venture's success started to taper off, and we were having trouble attracting more client family members. We had fun working together, so I asked her if she wanted to do sales for my coach-training school that had then been in existence for many years with great success. I was moving the school domain and the changing the school name, as I'd created a better name for the program, and I'd be keeping all of the materials intact.

She was excited to come onboard to spearhead sales. I operated the coaches-training school, and we were making a lot of money and serving a lot of people. I did the bulk of the work and asked her to focus on sales. We agreed that she'd be brought on as an independent contractor. In the beginning, she was really excited and handled sales very well. I changed the website to list her as co-founder because she said people wanted to speak with "the owner," and she needed a better title. That was a mistake I will always regret.

Over time, it became obvious to me that she was hiring a lot of people that I had to pay to do her sales work because she wanted to spend more time with her daughter and less time working. Her tasks included classes, question-and-answer sessions with students, creating materials for sales, and talking to student prospects.

But I was starting to see a large number of the leads that I paid a lot of money to acquire just sitting in our contact manager. When I asked her about this, she told me she wanted to bring on more sales and marketing people and have me pay them.

I found myself hiring sales and marketing people at her request. Money was going out the door, and she was doing less and less work. Although we still had revenue coming in, the profit margin was going down. I finally realized that I'd been way too generous in giving her 50% of the net profits of the program

— ridiculously generous. She was getting checks as big as $25,000 in a month. I informed her that this situation could not continue and that I would be the one leading the sales and marketing. I was certain that she would actually make more money with me in charge even though I was going to reduce her commission from 50% of net to 30% of net.

I explained to her that through my management of the profit margin, expenses, and sales, the bottom line would rise. Therefore, 30% of a higher bottom line would be more money for her with a lot less work.

She wasn't happy but eventually did accept this and continued on.

Everything happened exactly as I said it would. The bottom line increased, and her check was bigger, not smaller. She accepted this arrangement for about nine full months.

The day before I was leaving for a one-week trip to Aruba with my husband and she was leaving for some kind of a silent retreat in Mexico, we had our weekly phone chat. I asked her if everything was okay and if she needed anything from me. It was a cheerful conversation, and she said that everything was great and told me how much she appreciated me.

The next day, after she had left for Mexico, but before I'd left for Aruba, I got a letter from an attorney with whom she'd obviously been speaking for quite a long time. The letter said that she wanted to go to mediation and claimed she was a co-owner of the company — a partner *and* an employee — completely contrary positions. I won't get into all of the details, but over an 11-year period she sued me, my company, my website, and my program on 12 counts of anything and everything you can imagine, clearly grasping at straws. Eleven counts were thrown out in the actual trial before the judge would even hear the case.

A few months before the trial I realized that I held a lot of anger and resentment toward this woman. I had done more research on her and met a lot of people who knew her and told me she was mentally ill. She had told me that her dad had committed suicide in front of her when she was young. She had also said that she'd been planning on committing suicide at one point in her life, had blogged about this, and had the story on her website. She often talked about hearing angels and hearing voices speaking to her.

As a clinical psychologist, it was clear to me that something was not quite right with her. I took full responsibility for being blind to all the signals and for turning off my instincts that told me that I should not be doing business with her.

At one point late in the program, many of our students were asking for refunds because what they had been told on sales calls with her was not true to the program. She would tell them we included things that were never in the program. So, I was giving out a lot of refunds, as she was embellishing the program. Even though I spoke with her numerous times about this, something was off with her, yet I continued with her.

Hear me out. I am not pointing the finger of blame at her. Just like I didn't point it at my parents or at the boys who tried to set our box on fire. I am saying that I had all of the signs telling me to run — and I did not run. I believe that, for whatever reason, I made a conscious choice to wear blinders to who she was and how she was behaving.

The jury determined in minutes that was she was not my business partner. However, I spent hundreds of thousands of dollars to defend the case along with large amounts of time and energy. Money was wasted that would have gone to a foundation that I have for children with Reflex Sympathetic Dystrophy, but instead went to attorney fees.

I forgave her and let go before the deposition. As I unveil my process for you later, you will see how I actually forgave her and how I was able to sit in depositions and a five-day jury trial literally smiling at her and sending energy and love to her. I'm not just saying these words. I mean these words with all my heart. If we were ever to walk into the same room, I'd be happy to say hello to her and to maybe even hug her.

She was running from me during the trial. She made sure she didn't use the bathroom at the same time as I did and had her attorneys walk her back and forth, protecting her from me while she was the restroom. I, on the other hand, was hoping to have a moment with her just to say, "I love you." It may sound odd to you — and it *does* sound odd to me to be able to say that. I do love her. With all her imperfections, she is doing the best she possibly can. Just as we **all are.**

Next, I would like to journey into some family stories. I mentioned some things that occurred in my childhood, and I related something that occurred in my business. Forgiveness also shows up in my adult life in different ways with some family members.

Before we go any further, I'm going to request that you just check yourself and see how you are feeling about the information you've digested so far.

I will share with you my forgiveness process and how it unfolds. Some of it is not very pretty, so be prepared.

"Sorry" Seems to Be the Hardest Word

Sorry seems to be the hardest word

What I gotta do to make you love me
What I gotta do to make you care
What do I do when lightnin' strikes me
And a way to find when you're not there

What I gotta do to make you want me
What I gotta do to be heard
What do I say when it's all over
Sorry seems to be the hardest word
(That's right)

It's sad
So sad

It's a sad, sad situation
And it's gettin' more and more absurd
It's sad, so sad
Why can't we talk it over
Always seems to me
That sorry seems to be the hardest word

What do I do to make you want me
What I gotta do to be heard
What do I say when it's all over
Sorry seems to be the hardest word

It's sad
So sad
It's a sad, sad situation
And it's gettin' more and more absurd
It's sad, so sad
Why can't we talk it over
Always seems to me
Sorry seems to be the hardest word

Yeah

Sorry

What do I do to make you love me
What I gotta do to be heard
What do I do when lightning strikes me
Yeah
What have I gotta do
What have I gotta do
When sorry seems to be the hardest word

"Sorry Seems to Be the Hardest Word" —
Elton John

THE FIRST STEP IN FORGIVENESS is to take the time to retrieve your memories of people and experiences that you have not forgiven because they did not meet your need and caused you pain that still lingers in your mind, your heart and your body.

Here is my process to begin to open the forgiveness path within you.

I call it:

Recall

Remember

Realize

Recall means you actually allow yourself to sit with whatever has happened in your past and think about things that have upset you, angered you, or hurt you. Write them down in a notebook that you will use throughout our journey. You might write five today, and, in a few days, you might recall seven more and then another three and on and on. No matter how trite or traumatic, recall each experience and person that you have not forgiven — including yourself.

Remember that whatever happened to you was not personal. We all have circumstances, experiences, and people in our lives that we perceived as having "caused" us problems. Whatever they did is not about us. Whatever we perceived they did "to us" is not actually about us. If they acted out and did something they behaved as they did and we did not necessarily bring that upon ourselves. We need to let our memory of the experience be less personal and to understand that the way people behave is not about us. It is about those people and those situations, and we are just moving through this life encountering contrast so something new can be born. Contrast is noticing that when people behave in a way we don't expect this brings up emotion in us that we can experience and then release. This emotion is there for us to feel and experience and is part of life itself. Emotion is what makes human beings different from every other species so be grateful for the fact that you get to feel.

Realize that mistakes and errors happen in life. They don't happen *to* us — they happen *for* us. Although you might believe some incident you experienced seems like a "horrible" thing at that time, or this person is a bad person, and you may feel like a victim, staying angry only keeps you a victim. Letting go is a choice you can make. Life is made of experiences and feelings and emotions. You can choose what emotions to hold on to and which ones to let go of when you become conscious and present to the emotions you are experiencing. Our memories of things we judge to be "bad" may be unreliable and inaccurate. Our memories may not be fully correct. When you decide you can let go of any painful memory, then you are at *choice* — which is the first step to emotional freedom.

Let go or let it be.

— Terri Levine

THE GRUDGE

*"Grudges are for those who insist that they are
owed something; forgiveness, however, is for those
who are substantial enough to move on."*

Criss Jami, Salomé:
In Every Inch In Every Mile

I STARTED DATING MY HUSBAND when I was just 17
years old. He got to know me really fast and really
well. During that first year, a mutual friend irritated
me, and I shared the story with him. In his easygoing
voice, he said, "Can you change it?" I said, "No." He
went on, "Then there is no reason to think about it,
or to worry about it, and, least of all, to hold a grudge
about it." I remember thinking, *that's easy for you to
say,* because I didn't understand how to do this.

Many months later, when I was still really upset over this same person, he asked me, "Are you proud that you are really good at holding a grudge forever?" While his question hurt my feelings, I realized there was some truth in his question.

I still had no clue how to let a grudge go. I remained the Queen of Grudges well into my 40s. I was a personal-development coach; I'd studied clinical psychology, communication, and organizational behavior; my mentors were luminaries such as Zig Ziglar, Mary Kay Ash, Tony Robbins, Jack Canfield, Mark Victor Hansen, Joe Vitale, and others.

But I still hadn't mastered this idea of letting a grudge go.

I hired a life coach named Matthew Ferry. His approach was a very spiritual one, and he had a completely different take on life and life issues. I brought up my grudges, and he labeled them as "resentment" and told me I was self-righteous.

What? Me? Self-righteous?

He gave me examples of my behavior that showed how I *believed I was right* and how I went out of my way to justify and prove that I was right. He illustrated for me how this was hurting people I cared deeply about, like my husband and my father.

A great coach doesn't hold back. They speak the truth, and they hold up a mirror for you to see yourself in — even if the reflection is not always pretty. I digested the shock of accepting what he had shared with me and began to watch my behaviors, notice my language, and pay attention to my feelings.

He was right. I held grudges because someone or something made me feel as if I had done or said something wrong, and I always wanted to be right.

Wow! All these years, all these experts, all this schooling and training and no one had pointed this out to me! I couldn't believe it. This was so obvious, yet no one had shown this to me and brought this to light. Now I had the task of letting a grudge go. I tried everything. I asked people. I read books. I watched videos. I attended webinars. None of these things worked for me. I believe none of them worked for me because I didn't own them, and they weren't my own system. I have found that when I create a system that is my own and that is really in sync with my heart, I align with it better, and I stick to it better. So, I decided that I needed to create my own super-simple system. I needed to blend some of the processes I was learning and to create my own solution.

You will quickly see a pattern emerge here. I like to name things. I like three-step systems that are alliterations because I can easily remember them.

My system for grudge relief is Acknowledge, Accept, Allow.

Acknowledge is the first step, because until you figure out what is causing you to hold a grudge, you won't let go. All of the solutions others shared with me never required me to stop and really consider *why* I held grudges. When I understood and accepted that I held grudges because I wanted to be right, it was easy to move past the grudges.

Accept that the person or the circumstance is nothing more than just one fleeting moment among all the moments that make up your life. It simply is. They simply are. No need to judge. Who gave you or me the judgement robe? It is not up to us to judge anyone or anything. It simply *is*. Accept what *is*.

Allow yourself to know that you cannot change or control other people. You can't change their behaviors, and you can't manage other people and what they do. You can't control their actions. You can't do anything about what other people decide to do or not do. Let their choices and their behaviors be. I heard this expression once, and I use it a lot, "Not my circus, not my monkeys." To me this says, people do what people do. It is not my business how they behave. Focusing on their behavior is a choice. Why spend the precious time you have on this planet thinking about anything that isn't a good vibration that brings you joy?

Holding on to anger is like drinking poison and expecting the other person to die.

— Buddha

Grab your journal. Write down all of the grudges that you can think of that you have experienced over the course of your life, even if you think you have given up those resentments. I want you to write down every person you held a grudge against or an experience you held resentment about. This will help you open up to the forgiveness process I will be sharing as we get started on our forgiveness journey.

TRUE FORGIVENESS

"The truth is, unless you let go, unless you forgive yourself, unless you forgive the situation, unless you realize that the situation is over, you cannot move forward."

Steve Maraboli, Unapologetically You: Reflections on Life and the Human Experience

THERE WAS A TIME in my life when my behavior was so unlike me that I am a bit scared to even share it with you. However, I know sharing it will be beneficial so I will reveal it to you here. I often wonder what was going on in my mind. I wonder what I was thinking and why I behaved in this way.

I have asked these questions over and over again in hopes of understanding how I could get so off track and behave in a way that was so unlike me. At the time, I saw myself as happy and successful. I believed I was self-confident and loved myself, my family, my business, my friends, and my life.

I have spent the last years asking these questions over and over again to understand and to remember and to gain insight ...

I can feel the void that was there — the void that I had been living with for nearly a decade. Every minute of every day, I felt the burning, stabbing pain of Reflex Sympathetic Dystrophy. As my body tried to function with this intolerable pain, I was feeling a lack of self-love. I was taking more than 20 prescription medications a day and had recently gone through Ketamine infusions — and nothing was helping. I felt as if my life was over and that I was destined to live with this burning pain and pretend I was functional.

I hated the disease. I was mad at myself for getting this disease. I was mad at the world for creating this disease. I was mad at society for creating this disease. This "orphan disease" required medical treatments that weren't covered by insurance, and I woke up to that fact when the disease entered my body. At first, I desperately wanted to die, as I could not tolerate the pain of the disease.

Then, one day, the day I decided to end my life, somehow, I got a gift. Just when I was on the brink of ending my life, I realized that I could be a voice for children who had the disease, and I had the ability to raise funds for their treatment when insurance wouldn't pay. I realized my disease might be a gift instead of a curse, and I might be able to use my voice to help others. If I stopped my own pity party I could wake up and do something useful.

Along with my husband, I started a foundation dedicated to helping children and family members of children who were burning from the torture of the pain you feel when you have this disease. I was actually glad I was the one to be given this gift. I have a voice. I speak on stages to large audiences worldwide. I have a radio show and a TV show. I write books and blogs. I was in a position to educate people about this disease and fundraise for the children. I held no grudge. I didn't resent having this disease — although I must still admit I *was* depressed and often during intense flare ups of pain I still thought dying would be easier than living with so much pain. Focusing on the children and their pain and their need for funds drove me forward.

Something was still not quite right for me, although I pretended to be happy.

I don't think I consciously *knew* that something was missing — what with my pretend smile and fake "I'm OK" responses. How could I not be happy? I had an amazing marriage to a man whom I love and adore and who loves and adores me. I was surrounded by dear friends and beloved family members, and I was doing work that was making a real difference in the world. I enjoyed my client family members thoroughly. What could be missing? How could there be a void in such a life? Cars, three homes, vacations, and whatever I needed or wanted from a material perspective. What could be missing?

I was mentoring at CEO Space when my friend Paul suggested I help a man who needed some marketing advice. I love to help and share, so I decided to sit down with Paul's contact. I walked into the room with Paul to meet this man, and he seemed very disinterested. He was staring at his cell phone. I remember feeling a bit angry as I had so little time to meet with people who wanted my help, and here he was, ungrateful for my time. I was reading all kinds of things into the meeting. I typically did. I had a habit of judging people the second I met them. Soon, he looked up, and Paul asked if he could record the session. Paul turned on his phone to record the session, left it on the table, and exited the room.

I had another meeting in about 15 minutes and just wanted to get going. When I finally got the man's attention and asked what help he needed for his business, he stopped me. He told me that I couldn't help him, but he could help me. He told me that I was burning and that my legs were on fire. I thought he must be reading my mind because only people very close to me knew this. Soon he started talking to me about my pain. I noticed that his hand was shaking, and I recall wanting to run from the room. My intuition screamed at me to run, but I didn't. That choice defined what was to become the biggest lesson on forgiveness that I have ever received.

I know he asked to come to my side of the table at some point. I wanted to say "No," yet I nodded my head "Yes." He sat with me and talked about my "disease." Within a few minutes, he told me that he could not help me because I defined myself by my disease, and I was not willing to accept that the disease could leave my body or possibly already had. He turned to leave the room. As he reached the door, I felt that my last chance at health was walking away. I started crying. This was not like any cry I had ever experienced. It was a guttural and deep cry, and it sounded infantile.

He came over to me and held me while I cried. He told me he loved me unconditionally, and I recall thinking that it wasn't possible, as he didn't know me. Yet, something about this exchange was very comforting to me. I tried to pull away at one point, and he told me I wasn't done yet and pulled me back. He was right. I cried some more.

A few minutes later, my next appointment walked into the room. Paul came in to get his phone and told me he'd send me the recording. Out walked the mystery man.

I got on with my next appointment then had a few more meetings; later, I went out to dinner with a group. During dinner, I realized I hadn't taken any medication in many hours — yet felt very little pain. I thought that was odd. I went to bed that night not sure why my pain was diminished, but I was happy that it was.

When I woke up in the morning, I walked to the bathroom with almost no pain, and I felt happy and relieved. I went about my day of mentoring and activities, and at some point, saw the man who had spent time with me the day before.

I felt scared of him. I had no idea why. The day before I had allowed him to hold me in his arms. He had lovingly looked at me. He had shown me unconditional love - maybe for the first time in my entire life. I think, in retrospect, that this much love actually felt scary for me. I was not used to seeing anyone who was filled with such pure love and seemed to want nothing from me.

I asked other mentors to keep him away from me. He kept following me and smiling at me during an activity we were doing. I had no clue what his name was, and I was not comfortable with him or around him.

When it was time to conclude the activity and head home the next day, I still felt well. I was leaving in a few weeks to go to my home in Mexico. I'd always felt better in the warmth, so I was very optimistic about my health. I continued to take my medications yet had much less pain and noticed how much healthier I was feeling. I was happier and believed that my disease was greatly diminished all from spending only 9 minutes with this man. None of this made sense to me, and I felt some type of a miracle had happened that I could not explain.

About a month later, I was living in Mexico, feeling fairly healthy, and one of the CEO Space mentors asked if I would help him and another person help a student with branding and marketing. I am a helper, so I said "Yes."

I participated in a conference call with the business owner and the other people who were going to be working to help this man with his business. I didn't have a clue who the man was, and I offered help on the call then promised to create some things and send them to him. Within seconds of hanging up from this call, I received a private call from the business owner. He asked if I remembered him. I believed I'd never met him until the call we'd just had. Then he informed me that he was the same person I had the encounter with at CEO Space who helped me with my disease. His name was Brian.

Since I was feeling healthy and did think some "miracle" had happened in that room with my disease, I was happy to help him. We ended up speaking for hours on a Google Hangout. I did some work on his brand and marketing and sent that over to him. That was all the marketing and branding that I did for him as he saw that I needed more help with my health, and he wanted to assist me. He started giving me his time to assist me. He was back with me on another Google hangout for hours. Soon we were engaging in constant, long Google hangout chats. I was not helping with his business at all, and he was helping me with one breakthrough in my personal life after the next.

For a month or so, I was suddenly spending hours every day chatting with him. He lived in Hawaii, and I was in Mexico; there was a six-hour time difference. We would start to chat late at night, my time, and often I was up all night with him. I was missing out on sleep but finding myself drawn to the sessions with him. I noticed that I was feeling great, and I believed my disease was leaving my body. I loved this feeling and couldn't get enough of the man and what he called "spell break" sessions. During these sessions he would help me raise up frozen emotions from my past that had been stuck, or I thought were no big deal. Everything from things like the box incident, not eating, being hit by "Mr. Belt" and so much more. I came to realize that I had been holding onto these past experiences as if they were important, but they truly weren't. Each incident came up and was released. When the emotions were released, I became liberated from them and felt like I lost a ton of bricks. I could breathe easier and began to become happier, feel freer, and feel healthier. I gained clarity and peace. I had never experienced so much joy and bliss in my entire life.

I found myself talking about him to my friends in Mexico, and I believed he was some type of healer or miracle worker. I wanted to give back to him. I wanted to dedicate my time, energy, resources and my focus to him and for him. My heart was filled with gratitude for him and I felt as if he had breathed life into me. I told him that I was going to do his marketing and make him famous. I actually didn't know how to give back to him. I didn't know how to help and how to give. I wanted to give him millions of dollars but that didn't seem like enough. I just didn't know how to give back to someone who had given me my life and my desire to live back. I was deeply grateful and felt a lot of love for him.

I can still remember beginning to believe that he loved me unconditionally, that he had a magical gift for healing people, and that he truly felt unconditional love for all human beings. Sometimes his children came along on our Google Hangouts. They were very sweet and loving, and he was a beautiful father to them.

I would soon be leaving Mexico and heading back to CEO Space to mentor business owners. I was excited that the "spell breaker" would be there with me. I had been in Mexico, away from my husband, and I was to meet him at CEO Space. I hadn't had time to tell him about this man. I was excited for the two of them to meet, and I believed Mark would be grateful for Brian's *(The Spell Breaker's)* help.

I brought Brian to my hotel room to introduce the two of them. That meeting lasted only a few seconds, and it was surreal. Mark barely said a word and towered over Brian, looking angry. Brian said something like, "You would have to be blind not to see the changes in Terri." Mark looked pissed, and I quickly rushed out of the room with Brian. That exchange freaked me out — a lot.

I was confused about why Mark was so angry with the man who had pretty much cured me. I asked Mark, and Mark told me that he could see through Brian and thought he was a fraud. I felt Mark was sad that he had not been able to help remove the pain I had endured with Reflex Sympathetic Dystrophy while Brian had. Mark was jealous of my relationship with Brian and the emotional support Brian was giving me. I didn't know how to respond to Mark and support his feelings at the time.

I spent a lot of time with Brian at CEO Space, brought many people to him for spell-break sessions, and continued to have sessions with him while I was there.

I remember that Brian told me that I had been overworking (one of my patterns), and he said I should not hang out or relax at the bar — I should be in my room.

I went into rebellion mode. No one tells me what to do!

So, I showed up at the bar with my friend and business partner, Pete. Brian showed up at the bar, and I felt like a young girl again, about to be in trouble with my Dad. I believed that Brian was upset with me, which scared me. I was afraid that maybe Brian would not love me anymore. Maybe Brian would withdraw his seemingly unconditional love. I also felt that Pete wasn't digging Brian, and suddenly

I got scared. I have had a pattern my entire life of being scared of men. I was attacked by men when I was fifteen, and ever since then men have scared me. I don't trust them, and I am always expecting men to turn on me. This has been a lifelong pattern. Brian had shown me nothing but kindness, love, gentleness, and respect, yet my old patterns and fears showed up and felt fear.

I had a few friends who were also mentors, and I confided in them that I was afraid of Brian. They took me away from the bar, where Brian was chatting with Pete. I went off to listen to music. I could not figure out all night why I was afraid. I had never reacted to anyone so harshly, especially someone who had done so much for me and who had shown me such unconditional love.

Other mentors and "healers" and personal-development coaches who all wanted me to hire them began badmouthing Brian. Since I had already become scared of him, I took all this as evidence that

Brian was harming me in some way. I wanted these coaches' approval, and they were not giving it.

Finally, the day wound down. I went to a CEO Space friend who also knew Brian and explained that I was scared of him. I was shaking. We asked Brian to come to meet with me and my friend. During that exchange, I explained my fear. I clearly remember that Brian began to cry and laid his head on my shoulder. Even though I was afraid, part of me was not. I let him rest his head on my shoulder and felt his love again. I knew with all my being that he was feeling sad. Then I started to feel bad about running away from him. I ended up apologizing and questioning how I could have behaved this way, as this was so unlike my typical behavior. And I knew in my heart he had not hurt me and had not shown me anything but love.

At that time, I had no idea that my "odd" behavior was about to spiral out of control and would impact my life and my business — or how this "chance" initial meeting with Brian was going to bring forth life-changing moments.

Brian came to visit me at my home about a month later. My husband wouldn't spend time with him and couldn't stand having him around. It was all *really* awkward. We had spoken about him not liking Brian and not wanting him in my life. He wanted me well and knew that Brian was helping me, yet he didn't like him and felt he had some motive for helping me. We could not agree that Brian was simply being a loving, giving, and kind friend to me. I believe Mark was afraid that I was changing a lot, and this might at some point begin to impact our marriage. He never said these words, yet I came to believe he became insecure.

While Brian was at my home, he did a very long session with me. He was helping me go deeper to release some of my childhood emotions. All I could remember was my dad beating my feet, and I felt sad. I fell asleep on my sofa and was there, sound asleep, two hours later, when my husband arrived home. Brian had already left to walk to a movie.

Imagine Mark walking into his home. His wife was out cold. Brian was gone. Mark had never understood the work Brian did or seen a "spell break," and he was confused, angry, and upset. I could tell he wanted to confront Brian.

Finally, it was getting late, and Mark went up to bed. A few minutes later, Brian arrived back at my house. He and I chatted on the sofa for hours and then began more "spell break" sessions the next day.

During the sessions the next day, I felt this incredible urgency to go visit the Shaman named Radavie, who Brian had seen prior to arriving at my home. I wanted to go right then. I packed up some things, and off we went, driving from my home in Pennsylvania to North Carolina. I didn't tell Mark I was leaving until I had left. I texted him when I left. My husband came home to an empty house. I remember asking Brian to take me to her now and feeling this desperate need to get to her. He did as I asked.

Brian drove me away from my life and my family to go see Radavie. At the time, I wanted to go. I don't know what was going on in my mind. I just wanted to run somewhere fast and far. I had never done anything like this in my life or experienced this strong desire to run away. It was an odd feeling.

We drove. We ate. We talked. We laughed. We did more "spell breaks." The more "spell breaks" we did, the more I wanted to leave my world behind and be free of my life. I was confused. I couldn't figure out what was happening to me and where my mind was rushing off to. I was changing from the inside out, and, while I was happy, I was also feeling scared.

Finally, after several days, we arrived late one night in North Carolina. I gave Brian all my electronics so I could fully focus on my time with Radavie. I also lent him my car so he could visit his family in South Carolina. I began a solitary retreat, living in a small house called the "Apple House" and having sessions each day with Radavie.

I was instantly struck with the love that came from Radavie. For the first time ever, I was with someone who was ego-less and radiated so much love.

Each night, I journaled about my sessions with Radavie who took me back to heal my inner child. I quickly realized I had not been feeling any love for myself since acquiring the disease called Reflex Sympathetic Dystrophy. I had turned my focus to work and my foundation and had stopped allowing myself to feel and to think about myself. I opened up with Radavie in new ways and asked her within a day or so to ask my husband to come pick me up when our retreat ended. I asked her to tell Brian I was not going back to my home — or anywhere else — with him. I wanted to be back home with Mark.

By the time Mark came to pick me up, Radavie and I had become friends, not just Shaman and client. We walked. We talked. She helped me heal my childhood wounds, open up to self-love like I had never had, and forgive my parents for the wounds that they had inflicted.

I anxiously awaited my husband. When I saw him coming down the road in his rental car, I jumped in the car, and the two of us cried and cried together. Brian arrived hours later with my car, and I decided I needed a break from sessions with Brian, and I wanted to let him know this. I asked him to take a walk with me and left Mark and Radavie to chat.

I expressed my decision to him, and he and I sat on the path for hours, talking. I had no idea we'd been gone so long and when we came back to Radavie's home Mark was anxiously waiting and worrying about us being gone for hours.

Brian had driven in my car, and now needed to get back to Hawaii. Mark used some of our airline miles to book Brian's flight home. Since we were driving my car back to our home in Pennsylvania together, Mark gave Brian the rental car he had arrived in to take back to the airport to catch his flight.

We departed for the very long drive home and began trying to figure out together why I would suddenly pick up and run off without talking to Mark first. I was confused and couldn't figure out why I would do such a thing. Brian honored my request and left me alone for three days so I could begin to sort this all out. However, we were soon back to the routine of long late-night Google Hangout chats and more and more "spell break" sessions.

Within a month, Brian was back at my house to attend a meeting with my soon-to-be publisher in New York. Mark kept out of the way and tried to avoid him as much as possible. The man was sleeping in our home, and Mark was shocked that, after we had sent him back to Hawaii, he had found a way back into our lives.

After that visit, I realized Mark wanted me to keep away from Brian. Even though Brian was helping me and I had gone into very unlikely remission from Reflex Sympathetic Dystrophy, Mark didn't want Brian in our lives.

I felt sad and missed our chats, yet I knew I needed to create space away from him because I felt I needed to honor what Mark wanted and was being urged by Radavie to give myself time to process the work I had done with her. After I spoke at a dental conference one evening and was driving home late in the dark, I spaced out, lost track of what I was doing, and almost ran over some construction workers. I came home shaken up, and I texted Brian.

In a minute, he had me on a Google Hangout video chat and told me he was going to record it and have me show it to people to prove he wasn't influencing or controlling me as people kept claiming. My new way of acting without this disease was freaking out Mark and our friends. I was happy and free, and people were not used to me standing up for myself, speaking my truth and being independent, not co-dependent. On this chat, I was exhausted, and I was sleeping for a large part of the chat. After it ended, I sent the link to two of my friends, Mark, and two CEO Space fellow mentors. My friends were appalled. They told me Brian was controlling me, and I was acting like I was hypnotized. They told me he was nuts and begged me to not interact with him. The two mentors told me I had to stop associating with him because he was clearly using me. They said I had to stop these sessions, as they were not healing sessions, and I was being brainwashed. My husband got sick several times trying to watch the video and ended up in tears.

What no one realized is that I was exhausted and had nearly had a car accident that day. I was basically sleeping and could not speak on that call. It clearly was a mistake to record the call and to share it with people, but at the time I didn't realize that, and neither did Brian. On the call Brian was speaking and explaining our work together, and my head was down on the desk because I was mostly asleep. People thought he was hypnotizing me, and when he asked me a few questions and I would wake up and nod or agree they claimed that was because he controlled me to agree. Nothing could have been further from the truth. Their perceptions did not tell an accurate story. What they saw was Brian speaking and Terri mostly sleeping.

Several weeks went by, and I did not speak with Brian as much, because everyone's reaction scared me. Then I went back to mentor at CEO Space, and he was there. Our relationship actually grew this time, and I felt close to him. We talked for many hours, and I believed everyone was wrong about him and that only I really knew him. I dismissed other people's opinions about him. I saw a very beautiful and loving person helping me. He was also a great help to other people I referred to him during that conference.

When we said goodbye later that week, something told me I would never see him again. I have no idea why I felt this. Maybe a premonition. Brian had given me a check but told me he didn't have the funds to cover the check just yet. I am not sure if I forgot this information or didn't listen clearly or what happened. I gave the check to my husband to deposit and forgot to tell him to hold it until Brian had the funds to cover the check. A week or so later my husband told me Brian's check had bounced. I called Brian and was angry. Instead of speaking to him from a place of love, I came from a place of anger. I got on a Google

Hangout with him and was screaming at him. Soon I was saying some of the most horrific things that I have ever said to anyone in my life. I was yelling and totally lost control of myself. I was actually scared as I heard myself yelling. I had never spoken so loud or so harshly to anyone and was saying things that were unloving and made no sense. I found myself out of control. At the time, I didn't realize that I'd allowed other's opinions of him to affect me and that I'd now become fearful of him.

During that Google Hangout, both Mark and our nephew Charles came into my office and watched me say these awful things. I was mean and hurtful, and I was shaking and screaming. I had never acted this way in my life, and the anger scared me. When I was done, I would not allow Brian to speak, so, soon, he hung up.

I cut off my relationship with Brian after this event. I tried to go on without him in my life. However, this episode kept me up at night feeling incredibly guilty about why I had said such horrible things and acted so poorly.

Several weeks later, a friend came to visit me and Mark. Mark had spent time with her while I was working and confided in her that he didn't think I loved him anymore, and he felt that Brian was trying to get me to leave him for some reason. She was shocked and sad. She decided to try to talk to me. At the time I just thought she wanted to spend some girlfriend time alone with me at my shore place. I had no idea that Mark had shared confidential information with her about Brian, and she wanted private time to speak with me about how Mark felt.

She asked if she could stay longer and come to my shore home with me for a few days. We arrived at the shore, and she asked me about Brian. Then she asked me to have him do a session with her. He agreed, and while I was working, they had a session on her computer in my bedroom. Hours went by, and my friend emerged saying how great the session had been. She said that she wasn't going to pay him for it, but instead, she was going to get him TV coverage with her connections. I texted that information to Brian, and he texted me that he wanted to be paid for the session. I had expected her to pay for the session as well as that was the agreement.

My friend and I went to see the movie *In and Out*, and this took my mind off Brian. The minute we returned to my place Brian texted me to get my friend on a Google Hangout about the money she owed for the session. I did that. There were some words that I perceived were unpleasant between the two of them, and I ended up cowering in a ball curled up on the sofa. Finally, Brian asked her to put me in the video with her, and I don't recall what I said, if anything. I just remember that, at some point, he hung up because it was clear she was not going to pay him.

My friend spent hours with me showing me videos of people who lead cults and their behaviors, teaching me about mind control and gaslighting (telling people their memories were wrong), and showing me websites and having me read documents that showed that I was being controlled by Brian. She said he was a narcissist. I freaked out. How could I have let this happen to me? She told me she understood all of these behaviors because she grew up with a father like this. I felt totally out of control and became hysterical. After many hours, we went to bed.

At 5 am, I got up to go to the bathroom after only a few short hours of sleep, and my phone rang. Normally when I go to bed, I put my phone on airplane mode, but because of all the ups-and-downs of that evening, I had forgotten to do that. Brian's time zone, as I mentioned earlier, is six hours earlier. Often, he would leave me voicemails when I was sleeping, knowing that my phone would be in airplane mode, and I would retrieve them when I woke up.

When the phone rang and I saw that it was Brian calling, I could not believe he would call me at this hour. I was only surprised about him calling at this hour because of the argument with my friend. As I said this was normal but in my state of mind for some reason, I became angry about him calling. I threw my phone across the room. In the morning, I found that he'd left me a voicemail questioning the Facebook strategy I was using for him — one which had proven to work in the more-than 60 other businesses I was helping. I felt a lot of anger and left him a message saying I was blocking him everywhere and was going to let people know to keep away from him. I didn't realize at the time that he was simply inquiring to understand the Facebook strategy.

I had put clients and friends into his Conscious Creators group for many months. I had full access to the group. I messaged the group saying that he had controlled me, that he was a narcissist, and that they should run from him. I also had his Facebook access, and I posted on his page pretty much the same thing. I then went to my own page and posted that I had been mind-controlled for seven months. I didn't use his name on my page.

One of his ex-girlfriends contacted me, and then another. Even one of his ex-wives contacted me. Of course, they all had their own anti-Brian issues, as ex-wives often do. One of them actually went onto my wall and put up a very nasty post about him and then tagged the faculty and students of CEO Space so that anti-Brian slander now showed up on hundreds of people's walls.

As the weeks went on, someone close to me gained access to my Facebook account and began to post more and more horrible things about him directly on my page. I did nothing to prevent this or to stop it. I heard from people close to him that Brian was very sad, had taken to his bed, and had been crying for days, unable to understand.

My anger ran deep for about two months. I felt that I had been used and abused — so tricked, so fooled, so foolish, so taken advantage of — and I was scared of my own anger. One day I decided to do a forgiveness exercise by Colin Tipping called "Radical Forgiveness." I had been using this with my coaching clients for more than a decade; I had used this process myself before. I realized that I needed to use this process again. It is the only forgiveness process I have ever found that truly works. In fact, I find it to be somewhat miraculous. I was finally ready to let this unhealthy anger go.

I spent hours making sure the anger had left me, and soon I felt that I'd arrived at radical forgiveness, as I always had when I really, thoroughly allowed myself to go through Colin's process. I then shared the actual Radical Forgiveness document with both Mark and Brian. There was no reason for me to share the document. I believe I did so because I wanted Mark to know it was all over, and I wanted Brian to be aware that I was deeply and truly sorry.

Brian instantly asked to speak with me and told me he loved me. We went on a Google video chat, and I could barely look at him. I felt his hurt. A storm of guilt began to brew inside me that began to make me ill. I had to leave the chat several times to puke. He said he forgave me, and he loved me. Well, I believed him. I could not stop feeling horrible about what I had done to him and his business. I finally realized how I had allowed myself to listen to people who could not understand Brian's uniqueness.

Months went by. We chatted, did sessions, and texted. Mostly, I just felt horrified about my behavior. One night, I was about to break. I could not live with myself over this and could not figure out how to make it right — even though he said he'd forgiven me.

We went on a Google Hangout, and for hours we laughed, we cried, and I felt his forgiveness. He helped me release my guilt, and I felt happy again. Most of all, I realized that I wanted to clean up all the areas of my life in which I had not forgiven myself or others. The most important thing I wanted to do was to connect with others I had wronged and discover if they, too, would be forgiving.

I don't know about you, but I don't think the average person would have forgiven me. They certainly wouldn't be in a relationship with me right up until today, still choosing to give their help for hours, without ever being paid a dime. The average person wouldn't spend unpaid time helping me with the sensations I was experiencing from Reflex Sympathetic Dystrophy and helping me get to the deepest roots of what was holding the disease in place. The average person wouldn't be able to do it all from a place of love and caring and want nothing in return.

What is this lesson Brian taught me, shared with me and gave me? Brian showed me true forgiveness. I nearly destroyed his reputation and his career. I tried to hurt him in any way possible and destroy his business. The man who showed me nothing but unconditional love and gave me hours and hours of love and care for free. This beautiful human being. This man who comes from pure, unconditional love.

To truly forgive completely and continue to be in my life as my dear friend, maybe my best friend who really has my back, even today, who shows me unconditional love, who cares for and about me, who gives to me, and who is always there for me despite what I have done to him, is the ultimate forgiveness lesson.

I think when someone shows up with such pure love and light to others who have never seen this, those people run. They tried to get me to run, and I allowed myself to do just that. I happily, fully accept and appreciate his kindness, help, friendship, caring, compassion, and loving. He has actually shown me forgiveness and allowed me to become a forgiving person.

Two people remember the things they do to each other. If they stay together, it's not because they forget; it's because they forgive.

— *Demi Moore in Indecent Proposal*

Who do you want to clean up with? Which people have you wronged? Be honest here. Put their names in your journal. If they are deceased, write them a letter asking for their forgiveness and then see and feel them releasing you. Thank them. Send them love and light, and move on, knowing you have made it right.

If they are still living, my forgiveness process can help you change your life. Write down the names of all the people you want and need to apologize to — for your benefit.

Forgive Me?
Forgive Me Not?

*If I have harmed anyone in any way either
knowingly or unknowingly
through my own confusions, I ask their
forgiveness.*

*If anyone has harmed me in any way either
knowingly or unknowingly
through their own confusions, I forgive them.*

*And if there is a situation I am not yet ready to
forgive,
I forgive myself for that.*

*For all the ways that I harm myself, negate,
doubt, belittle myself,
judge or am unkind to myself through my own
confusions,*

I forgive myself.
— **Buddhist Prayer of Forgiveness**

FORGIVENESS BEGINS WITH forgiving yourself even if the person you apologize to doesn't accept your apology. I will repeat this, so you really, deeply internalize this. You forgive yourself. You let whatever you did, said, or felt be dismissed and forgive yourself for being a human being. We're all trying to be perfect with all our imperfections.

We cannot control other people's behaviors. We can control only our own actions. If I have wronged you and am now realizing it and apologizing, I do not need you to accept my apology or to accept me. Knowing that I am truly sorry is enough for me to be able to love myself and continue to grow. I will let it go and love you and myself even if you don't let my apology in.

This is actually a very deep lesson, and I discovered a process for this. Many years ago, my niece, Sarah, who I always felt very close to, acted in a way that I righteously perceived to be "wrong." Instead of loving her unconditionally, I did not stand by her and support her. I hurt her — a lot. She decided to shut me out of her life. I felt sad, but I did not communicate my feelings to her, nor did I seek to understand her behaviors and actions. Time passed; soon she was busy with her new marriage, and our lives moved apart.

I thank Brian because he opened me up to understand how I could forgive myself, how I could be forgiven, and how I could forgive others. I thank Radavie, who showed me unconditional love. I thank Colin Tipping for his Radical Forgiveness process.

These people and these processes led me to finally go to Sarah and see if this beautiful woman, loving wife, and adoring mother could actually forgive her Aunt T. I reached out, and she accepted my invitation to talk.

I often recall that conversation — two adults being transparent and honest and deeply communicating through hurt and sadness and a big lapse in time. I asked Sarah for forgiveness even though I knew there was a good chance she might not forgive me. Sarah was incredibly mature and very loving. She did forgive me. My heart was beyond joy-filled. I love this woman with my heart and soul, and I had behaved in a manner that did not support her. My own judgment and self-righteous behavior had interfered with someone I love beyond words.

One thing I have discovered over and over again in life is that the Universe loves to test you. Very quickly after we began rebuilding our relationship, my sister, Sarah's mom, sent me a text that she no longer wanted to speak to me for some perceived wrong. The text was very strong and very clear. I backed away, letting her know I loved her. I forgave her. I said I was sorry and that I'd always be here loving her as her sister if she ever wanted or needed me.

I then went through the process I had created to make sure every bone in my body and every thought in my head was sending love and forgiveness to Lynn. I once again used the Radical Forgiveness process. Once I went through these processes (don't worry — I will take you through the processes shortly), I realized that forgiveness was happening for me without any effort. It had become natural. I also realized that, since I had opened myself up with forgiveness, I was loving people without conditions. That is a very beautiful way to live.

I am not sharing the processes at this moment. Why? I want you first to get super-clear on who and what you want to forgive and why you want to forgive them. I want you also to know who you want or need to seek forgiveness from. You simply can't skip these steps and expect these processes to work.

Look at your journal. Who do you want or need to forgive? What experiences are you willing to release? From whom will you plan to ask for forgiveness? Have you made peace with those you have lost through the steps in the last chapter? What do you want to forgive yourself for?

Seriously, unless you take the time and put in the energy to answer all of these questions, you will only be putting a Band-Aid on forgiveness. I want to transform your life — not just inform you about forgiveness. Will you allow me to do this with you and for you? You hold this book and, soon, the keys to my process. You need to be willing to take action and be part of my forgiveness-coaching process to make the changes you seek in your life, health, wealth, and happiness.

Forgiveness in Minutes

Please forgive me; I know not what I do
Please forgive me; I can't stop loving you
Don't deny me this pain I'm going through
Please forgive me, if I need you like I do
Please believe me; every word I say is true
Please forgive me; I can't stop loving you
"Please Forgive Me" — Bryan Adams

COLIN TIPPING CREATED a Radical Forgiveness worksheet, which was the process I used to forgive Brian. I acknowledge his work and appreciate his process. I recommend and continue to use his process. In addition to that process, I also created my own process. I was creating this process just for myself. I had no idea I was going to create a process that would go beyond me.

A client texted me one day and said she had an emergency and requested a few minutes of my time. She quickly told me that her business partner had taken money from the business, almost ruining it. She also said he was destroying her reputation, and she was very angry with him. She said she was so angry that she wanted to publicly lash out and ruin him. Interesting. I recalled these same feelings from when I was angry with Brian. I totally related.

I let her vent this all out with me, and we stayed on the phone for hours. I asked her if she wanted to remain angry or if she wanted to love him and herself, forgive the experience and him, and return to money-making business activities from a place of love, peace, and kindness. I also told her that I would not judge her decision and would be with her, no matter what. She said she needed to sleep on this idea. I also understood this, as I had not been ready to forgive Brian right away, either.

When we hung up, I sent her the *Ho'oponopono* Hawaiian practice of reconciliation and forgiveness. I also asked her whether she would be open to the Radical Forgiveness worksheet by Colin Tipping. She agreed to do both. I will share the worksheet with you shortly. In the meantime, I will tell you that I asked her to repeat this meditation for the next few days whenever she felt upset with her former partner or the situation, or with herself. I also told her I loved her unconditionally and would be here for her.

The next day, she phoned me and told me that something had shifted and that she didn't understand how repeating the words *"I Love You, I'm Sorry, Please Forgive Me, Thank You"* could make a difference. I explained to her that *Ho'oponopono* means "to make right or to rectify an error or a mistake." When something or someone troubles you, or when you experience fear, anger, or sadness, your subconscious is associating a situation, action, or person in the present with something that happened in the past. Then your emotions take over.

Ho'oponopono allows you to ask that, in each moment, your errors in thoughts, words, deeds, feelings, or actions be cleansed. You are releasing past memories and experiences and trying to find a place where you are no longer willing to store them in your cellular memory. Whatever doesn't serve you and make you happy, vibrant, peaceful, and healthy is what you let go of when you repeat *Ho'oponopono*.

Whenever you don't feel peace or forgiveness, I believe you are out of balance. You can go inside yourself and release any feelings or memories that aren't pleasant and that don't add to your well-being and the greater good.

She asked me if it was really this simple. She said she had done the Radical Forgiveness worksheet and was using the prayer, and it seemed as if a miracle was happening.

I decided I would share my entire forgiveness process with her. I had no idea the impact it would have on her business and life and, later, the impact it would have on others as I shared the process with more people.

Before I reveal the steps to you, I just want you to begin with *Ho'oponopono* and nothing more.

Sit quietly and think of what you are remorseful about. Take on any problems — even if you didn't create them — and choose to be sorry for them. As an example: one of my client family members had a major computer crash. She was angry with herself for not backing up her system. She was upset that her life partner didn't suggest backing it up. She was angry at the computer as well. She had been holding on to this energy for five days. I asked her to notice this — just to *notice* this. I asked her to simply notice and bring this into her awareness.

Right now, jot down everything that you are remorseful or angry for — regardless of when it happened, why it happened, or what happened.

Here is the *Ho'oponopono* practice.

1. Say I'M SORRY. When you say it, believe that you are responsible for everything in your life. Show remorse that something within you caused this — no matter what it is.

2. Say PLEASE FORGIVE ME. Hold that remorse, and now ask for forgiveness.

3. Say THANK YOU. Thank the Universe for forgiving you.

4. Say I LOVE YOU. Tell the Universe, yourself, your experiences, all human beings, the trees, the rivers, your obstacles…. Just say it — and really mean it as you say it.

Start saying the words *"I'm sorry, Please forgive me, Thank you, I love you"* over and over and over again. This is a meditation to move you into forgiveness. It is very simple. It is very effective. It is very powerful.

The next process that I will ask you to do is the Radical Forgiveness worksheet that I am including in the appendix to this book. Colin Tipping created this, and I am very grateful that he did. This is truly the deepest way to forgive. I have never found another tool on the planet that comes close to this one for allowing true forgiveness. So be certain that you look at the appendix and you actually take time to do the worksheet on each and every person and each and every experience that you choose to forgive. Sometimes I have spent hours doing a worksheet on just one situation, forgiving either myself, a circumstance, or another person.

So why did I add to these processes?

I found that blending in some elements actually made these processes work much faster for me and activated the words and writings to have more meaning. I believe that when you add my process together with the *Ho'oponopono* process and the Radical Forgiveness worksheets, you will expedite your results and feel forgiveness much faster.

Now let's get into my process. It is simple and highly effective. You will add to the prayer once you have done the worksheet in the appendix so you can actually begin forgiving everyone, everything, and, most importantly, yourself.

I will list the steps here and then take you on a deep journey through each in the coming chapters.

Step 1: Thoughts

When you think of the experiences or people whom you have not yet forgiven, know that your thinking impacts your mind, your body, and your emotions. The first step of the process isn't just thinking "I'm Sorry" — it is accepting that your thoughts have influenced your emotions. It is time for you to change your thoughts, so you can shift your emotions.

Step 2: Fears

Fear of any kind sets up barriers and is usually based on illusions. We believe these illusions and treat them as if they are factual. Unless you realize you have fears, you cannot release them. It is time to move through your fears and no longer turn away from them. You can't begin to ask for forgiveness unless you are ready to look fear in the face and have no fear of what might happen.

Step 3: Choices

Choices are demonstrated by your actions. You make choices in each and every moment. It is a choice to say "Thank you" for whoever or whatever it was that just forgave you. It is a choice to wallow in life-destroying activities and stay in your anger and misery or actively and enthusiastically shift to loving and supportive thoughts.

Step 4: Commitments

I want for you to fully commit to living your best life right now. That means that, in every single moment you are on the planet, you are healthy, wealthy, and happy, with clear intentions and the willingness to love. When you say, "I love you," promise your body, your mind, the Universe, every person, and every experience that you will feel love.

Are you ready to open up to living a life in which you are truly free and filled with self-love and universal, unconditional love? I know you are! Let's go!

THOUGHTS

*"Remove the negative thought and watch your
entire life change."*
— Terri Levine

To TRULY EXPERIENCE FORGIVENESS, you must accept that you can't spend any time thinking negative thoughts. Why? Thoughts cause your body to have a full-blown response. If someone mentions "…nails on a chalkboard…" I shudder. Thoughts influence every emotion. Think about the people and experiences you want to forgive.

Most people, in my experience, work on changing their emotions. They go to therapists and life coaches, read self-help books, and take personal-development courses to change their emotions. I believe this is a waste of time and energy because when we change our thoughts, our emotions change with them.

I am writing this as I sit on my balcony overlooking the ocean. This is my favorite place — I have nicknamed it "My Happy Place." I feel positive and happy. I'm smiling as I view the sunshine and the ocean waves. I smell the ocean air and feel the sea breeze on my body. These very positive thoughts are producing emotions.

When those boys tried to set our box-tent on fire, I felt the "fight-or-flight" response of perceived danger. Ever since that event, if I spent even just a minute thinking about it, my emotions would instantly be activated. Whatever you have not yet forgiven is causing automatic physiological responses in your mind and body. You are being triggered and might not even realize this. The thoughts are controlling you because you are not controlling the thoughts.

The human brain looks for danger. That is how our brains are programmed. We focus consciously and unconsciously on potential dangers around us. We're trying to solve problems all the time. When your mind is focusing on the negative, your body follows, with negative experiences being activated in your emotions. Your imagination confuses reality with fantasy.

As an example, when they boys set fire to the boxes and I escaped, that was over. Yet, as an adult, if I thought about this for a moment, I felt scared. Why? I was safe. There was no box. There were no boys. There was no fire. I was safe. Yet, my body and my mind held on to that experience and automatically triggered a chemical response that put a huge stress on my mind as well as my physical body.

As you notice your thoughts, you can become aware of how they can create a downward spiral that never ends.

This is why I repeat what I once read by Peter McWilliams: ***"You can't afford the luxury of a negative thought."***

If you want to live a delicious and wonderful life, you must choose thoughts that will support the results you want. Holding grudges and being angry and upset with yourself, others, or life experiences are not healthy choices. Remember the words of John Milton: *"The mind is its own place, and in itself can make heaven of hell, a hell of heaven."*

I have come to believe that my pain from Reflex Sympathetic Dystrophy was caused by holding on to the belief that I was sick. I told my mind how sick I was. I focused on that thought over and over again, as did my medical team. When Brian told me that I was holding on to my disease and it was forming my self-image, I began to notice my thoughts about my body, my health, and the disease I believed I had. I had to admit that this *was* my dominant thought and had become my unconscious belief. It was a pattern of thinking that I had not even recognized. I was putting emotional stress on my own body with my thoughts. I was adding to my body's physiological stress, too. I was literally making myself ill with my own thoughts.

FEARS

No sleep today
Can't even rest when the sun's down
No time
There's not enough
And nobody's watchin' me now
When we were children, we'd play
Out in the streets just dipped in fate
When we were children, we'd say
That we don't know the meaning of
Fear, fear, fear,
Fear, fear, fear
We don't know the meaning of…
When we were children, we'd play
Out in the streets just dipped in fate

When we were children, we'd say
That we don't know the meaning of
Fear, fear, fear,
Fear, fear, fear
We don't know the meaning of...

"Fear" — One Republic

I FIND THAT THE COMMON thoughts related to being angry or upset and holding grudges come from fear. As you think about something or someone you haven't yet forgiven, notice what you feel. Are you angry? Are you outraged? Do you feel hurt? Are you feeling sad? Are you feeling upset? Are you holding on to any guilt? What about resentment? Try hostility. Hurt? Maybe even depressed?

I found myself strongly feeling these things in regard to Brian. These were the emotions I felt, and they surfaced over and over again in my thoughts, which would then trigger all kinds of emotions.

When I decided to look beneath those thoughts and into what I was afraid of, I noticed the overall fears were apprehension mixed with grief or loss. You might have other fears. Fears might show up as anxiety or apprehension. All of these fears stem from emotions that are caused by thoughts you might not even be aware that you are thinking. Those thoughts, which cause matching emotions, might not even be rational.

In my case, Brian had forgiven me. Why was I angry? Outraged? Hurt? Sad? Upset? Guilty? Resentful? Hostile? Depressed? In retrospect, those were thoughts not based on truth that caused emotions that weren't rational and caused me to make some very poor decisions at that time. I was so scared by my thoughts, which, in turn, impacted my emotions, so I did not act logically.

When we hold on to fearful thoughts without noticing them, they can become almost addictive, because those thoughts are habits that get ingrained into our brains. One of my thoughts that caused an emotional response was my self-righteousness. I had to be right. I had to prove I was smarter than others. This was my unrecognized pattern until I discovered this forgiveness process that I am sharing with you. I would do or say anything to prove I was right.

I am guessing this need I had to prove that I was right came from being compared to my very brilliant sister who got A's in school. She was the "smart" one, and I felt like I was the dumb one. I had to show and the world that I also knew things, so I had to be right — even if that meant making someone else wrong. It was eye-opening when one of my coaches showed me my fear of being wrong or looking stupid. If I continued with this persistent thought and fear that I might not look smart and kept trying to prove that I was right, my life would not have been so extraordinary. Many family, friends, and client family members would not have embraced me. I would not have been able to manifest the close and loving relationships I have.

I had to learn this lesson and allow myself to admit that I was wrong to my niece, Sarah. I no longer was willing to accept my fear of looking dumb and being wrong. I admitted I was wrong, opened up my heart, and asked for forgiveness. I did not worry about my fear of her thinking I was stupid or even rejecting me. I made a very conscious choice to create my own reality with my thoughts and not to let fear guide me. Thoughts do create your reality. I decided to put my focus on loving Sarah and not worry about any response she might give me. It was okay if she rejected me or if she thought I was wrong. I decided I would replace fear with love — love for Sarah, and love for myself. The vibration of those thoughts led me to ask Sarah for forgiveness.

CHOICES

We all have a choice

to live a lie

or be ourselves

to laugh and cry

or to follow someone else

to look up and smile

or bow down and frown

to walk the whole mile

or take off our crown

We have a choice

to shout out loud

or chant a whisper

to fly through the clouds

or to be blown like paper

to conquer our fear
or hide in the shadow
or wise words hear
or be thrown out the window
We all have a choice
to climb our highest mountain
or fall into our deepest hole
to drink from life's fountain
or live life like a troubled soul

"Choices" — Allen Steble

OUR LIVES ARE FILLED with choices in every moment. Most of the time, we go about our days in an unintentional, mindless way. As an example, when I was overweight, I ate without thinking. I opened the refrigerator and ate. I ate all the food on my plate. I had seconds. I ate unhealthy foods. I just ate, without making clear, intentional choices.

I learned to be conscious of my food choices. I stopped dieting, lost weight, and kept it off. How? I realized that dieting was not a solution that worked for me, as I had been dieting on and off since I was about 15. Instead, I decided I would self-coach, based on my choices of eating healthy and having a healthier lifestyle. I simply used the intention of eating mindfully and changed the way I ate. Before I put a morsel of food in my mouth, I would check on my choice. If I was going to eat a cookie, I'd check to see if this was the very best cookie on the planet. Was it worth it to eat the cookie — or more worth it to be able to fit into a smaller size? Before I started conscious eating, I didn't understand that I had the option of thinking before I ate. My thoughts were unconscious, and I ate without being fully present.

I also made choices to eat poorly because I didn't feel I was worth it. Maybe I didn't believe I was good enough. Interesting, yes? In retrospect, it was similar to my fear of not being smart enough. This "unworthy" thinking was not a conscious choice. I had no idea I was thinking this way until I decided to be mindful and to actually put conscious thoughts about food into my brain.

How does this relate to forgiveness? *Forgiveness is a choice.* Your thoughts are running your life. They have turned into triggers and emotions and are based on fears that you have. When you choose to think differently, you will change your emotions, release your fears, and allow in what you truly deserve. Holding onto anger, resentment, guilt, and grudges undermines you and brings negativity into your world.

When we are children, we develop a lot of beliefs. We are *bad.* We are *not good enough.* We are *unlovable.* We are *undeserving.* We are *unworthy.* In my case, I believed I'd never be as smart as my sister, Lynn, so I wasn't ever going to be loved as much as she was. I was never going to be good enough in my parents' eyes. She would be loved more because she ate all her food at the dinner table. I had to sit there for many hours, staring at food I could not eat, so I was never going to be loved the same way my sister was.

Sounds ridiculous, right? Well, I held those thoughts until I intentionally decided to choose new thoughts.

Your thoughts determine your emotional and physical well-being. Your thoughts might be illusions. Mine were. My parents really did love me. While I might not be book-smart like Lynn, I am a brilliant business owner, loyal friend, and loving wife, who managed to get a bachelor's, a master's, and a PhD, and who has published dozens of bestselling books, created eight successful companies, helped more than 5,000 business owners, become an expert on major media, and who does highly paid keynote speeches all over the globe. I'd say that I am pretty smart in my own right. I have also figured out a formula for making a lot of money and sharing my money with my foundation, friends, and family.

The attachment to my thoughts was not a mindful choice — just as being angry with the boys, with my parents, with my sister, my niece, or Brian was not a conscious decision. When I chose to detach from the thoughts and made a choice to let go of all my fear, all my old programs, my negative thinking and my triggers I moved forward. I literally moved through my fears. I stopped pretending they weren't there and trying to turn away from them. Instead, I made clear and intentional choices about how I wanted to feel. When I did this, I felt joy and excitement. I noticed I felt more confident — even courageous. I showed up as the very best version of Terri in every situation.

In this moment, you need to make a choice to be forgiving and loving towards yourself and every person, every circumstance that you have not yet forgiven. Right now, be conscious. Be present. Be mindful. You'll be able to see what has happened in your life as well as what will happen in your life. Will you see it filled with thorns or with wonderful gifts — the way I saw having a disease? I first saw having a disease as a death sentence. Once I stopped the pity party and realized I had a voice and could help kids with Reflex Sympathetic Dystrophy, everything changed. Whatever you choose to think, you will feel.

Thoughts effect our feelings. Choose your thoughts carefully as they will determine your emotions.

Pick your head up right now. Look around at your environment. You can find fault with it, or you can decide to find the positives and celebrate them. I can look out at the ocean today and tell you it looks angry, or I can see it as beautiful waves that show off its awesome power. I can look out at the beach and see it as white and sandy and sparkling, or I can see it as hard and cold. I get to decide. I am in control. I can make a choice.

Having a choice means you *decide* to focus on what is working and what is going right. You truly are able to forgive fully and with intention. I am not talking about "positive thinking" at all. When I became a coach, many decades ago, I had already studied personal development since I was 16. I thought I had to practice "positive thinking" to enjoy life and that I needed to imagine things positively, no matter what. I don't believe that anymore, and coach training changed my thinking and my life.

I am asking you to make a choice to focus on what *is* positive. Don't confuse this with *convincing yourself* that things are positive. I prefer to notice things that are positive. Look at my relationship with my sister. I could try to fool myself to thinking positive thoughts about the fact that my only sibling never wants to speak to me again. That would not be reality. Instead, I choose to focus my thoughts on the reality that is positive: I love her. I wish her a magnificent life, filled with everything she desires. I accept her for not wanting me in her life. I honor her. My thoughts about her are positive *and* real. It is a matter of choice to accept each moment, each person, each experience — and yourself — as just perfect. So, no — I don't practice "positive thinking." That only highlights the gap between where I am and where I want to be. I accept where I am and find positive aspects of that experience or situation.

How Do You Actually Learn to Love Yourself?

"Forgiveness is an inside job. Forgiveness comes from the deepest love of and for one's self."

— Terri Levine

SHARING MY OWN STORY and being vulnerable with you, my reader, would not be complete unless I left you with some guidance for self-love. I have been on my own self-healing journey for a few decades in order to discover this process.

As I created this process for myself, I began to share elements of it with clients, family, and friends.

I did some Facebook Lives, sharing my journey and the process as well. Soon, people were insisting I help others with this inner guidance. This is why I decided to write this book.

You must be willing to feel pain and take responsibility for your feelings. All feelings are informational, letting us know whether we're loving ourselves or abandoning ourselves, or if others are being loving or controlling.

I ask you to sit quietly and begin some deep diaphragmatic breathing. Mindfully follow your breath and become fully present in your body. Allow feelings to come, and lovingly and compassionately and willingly embrace all feelings. Remember that no one is responsible for your feelings other than you. You get to choose each feeling in each moment.

I have discovered that loving yourself will improve every single thing in your life. I am talking about your ability to manifest your dreams, improve your self-esteem, enhance your health, well-being, and ability to love, deeply connect with others, and create loving relationships. I believe that self-love allows you to live a fulfilled and joy-filled life.

Sit quietly breathing and reflecting, and notice what comes up. Is there any shame? Loneliness? Depression? Emptiness? Anxiety? Pain? Just *notice* what is showing up.

The key to self-love is allowing yourself to connect with your own inner guidance, your own higher self, and learning to be open about actually loving yourself. Be open to answers that may show up.

Once you open your heart, words and images will float to you, as well as the answers you are seeking. Take time each day to close your eyes and breathe deeply. Ask yourself how you can be more loving, kind, gentle, and in love with yourself. Allowing yourself to hear those answers will give you the information you're seeking.

As you go through each day, notice when you are thinking thoughts that are not coming from self-love.

Notice when you speak words that are not filled with self-love. The more you notice, the more you can quickly make shifts — until you actually *do* fall in love with yourself.

Just a few days ago, Brian and I were having a conversation, and I had to change a bandage on my foot. Right now, I have a large wound on my foot which is extremely painful and is bringing Reflex Sympathetic Dystrophy sensations with it. Whenever I change the bandage, it creates additional sensations. When I changed the bandage, I didn't even realize that I was yelling out loud at myself, cussing myself out, and definitely not loving myself. I also didn't even remember that Brian was still able to hear me talking out loud.

He gently reminded me that I wasn't loving myself. He asked me, "What if you had an infant child who you'd accidentally left in its crib for a short time? If the infant had pooped its diaper and the poop had gotten everywhere, would you have screamed and yelled at that baby?" Of course, I said I would not.

He asked how I would've responded. I told him I would've talked softly to the baby and quickly cleaned up the baby while taking full responsibility. I would have told the baby how much I loved him or her. I would have held and comforted the baby. I would have promised the baby I would not leave him or her alone again, and I probably would have lain with the baby. He asked me what it would be like if I had that same kind of love for myself?

That incident helped me immensely, and I wanted to share it with you. Instead of being angry at my foot for the pain that it was creating and for the fact that it had a wound on it, I am loving my foot, appreciating my foot, and treating that foot as if it were that tender baby whom I truly love, since it is a part of me, and I must show it self-love.

By showing my foot self-love, I am increasing my own self-love. No matter what you are not loving about yourself, your behaviors, or even your own body parts, it is time to sit, quietly breathing, and remember the story about loving a baby. Look inward and allow yourself to love your thoughts, your behaviors, *and* your own body parts. I don't care what your body looks like right now — big, small, whatever it might be. Turn to it and love it as if it were that baby — because, actually, it is.

As I complete this chapter, I know you may be thinking *Is that all there is? Just sitting and breathing and allowing myself to love myself?* Notice that all of these things take practice. I didn't realize I was not loving myself, and luckily, Brian happened to hear my conversation with my foot. Practice, practice, practice — and decide and choose to love yourself always and all ways.

WHAT NOW?

I WOULD LIKE YOU TO RE-READ this entire book. Use your highlighter, use your journal, and then do all of the exercises. Make sure you do the prayer that I gave you, do the worksheets, and use the processes that I've included. And I mean all of them, including sitting quietly and diaphragmatically breathing.

Don't rush through any of these processes. One worksheet may take you hours, and you may need to do it again and again, until you truly feel forgiveness — with not a speck of anything else left over. The more deeply you honor yourself and allow yourself to go through these processes, the more you will find you truly change from the inside out.

Even though I am a coach and a psychologist, I realize that both of those modalities don't change people from the inside. The processes I have shared with you are transformational and allow you to change from the inside out. You are not just saying positive words and changing your language — you truly are transforming, like me, because I am you and you are me. You can choose to change from the inside out. When you forgive, you heal yourself by forgiving yourself, and we are all connected as one. Therefore, you actually transform me, too. If you feel more self-love, then I, too, have more love. This is how people change and how the world changes. Transformation is change. As you forgive and love, you change.

Imagine for a moment if everyone we came in contact with loved themselves and truly loved each other. Imagine everyone on the planet coming from self-love and true, deep forgiveness. I think we would experience life — for the first time — with true connection and really understand the oneness of the universe.

As you truly get to know yourself, you will set yourself up for greater success in all areas of your life.

Awaken to the experiences that have happened in your life and be grateful and appreciate everything that has happened along your journey.

As I began to release and let go of everything, including the experience with the boys, my parents, my sister, my niece, and Brian, I released pain, sorrow, and disconnectedness. Say the prayer, complete the worksheets, and begin to breathe. You will realize that everything happens for a reason, that everything is truly a lesson and a gift, and that it has all unfolded just the way it is supposed to.

Keep your attention focused on allowing everything that has happened to be forgiven. Be present to truly listen and focus your concentration on forgiveness and love.

You are on the right path. You are beautiful and perfect, even with all your imperfections. I see you! I love you! You are a beautiful, shining diamond, unconditionally loved and supported more than you know.

Be willing to work through anything and anyone that needs forgiveness. Be committed to be a forgiving and loving person because that is the highest power you can ever achieve. Living a life with love, forgiveness, and compassion will allow you to have the most delicious life ever.

Trust everything that is happening and has happened in your life and forgive and love everyone.

Just yesterday, as I was working to complete this book, I was chatting with someone, and some other friends noticed me chatting with her. After she left, they couldn't wait to tell me all the bad things she had done to them and how much they loathed her. I told them that perhaps she had done some things to me, too, but that I chose to forgive her. I chose to love her. No one gave me a judgment robe. I'm sure I've done some things in my life that aren't great, either. I asked them to be still and quiet for just one moment and to realize that there is a oneness and connectedness to all living things and all living beings. I asked them to look at the world from inside her shoes. I asked them to have a little bit of courage and truly open their hearts with self-love. I asked them to step outside of their own beliefs and views that people do things solely to hurt them or to be mean or to be bad. I asked them to believe that each person is doing the best they can in the moment.

I don't know if they were willing or unwilling to do the things I was asking of them. I hope that you are willing to. If more of us stay real and loving, we can shift this world to a new paradigm. We can bring about a new level of consciousness, filled with love and peace. I know you've heard the saying, "Be the change you want to see in the world," and I want to remind you of that.

Allow yourself to be loving and forgiving and to step willingly into love and forgiveness. Each of us is a unique being, and we each have our individual truth. It is time to honor your own truth, to come from self-love, and to heal your own life, so that you can love others more fully. Trust in the Universe — trust that everything is absolutely perfect. You are here to learn and to connect and to live more fully. This book was written to help you let go and be more conscious. I hope you will become more aware of your higher self and release those aspects of yourself that no longer serve you.

This book will really help you grow unless you resist changing. The steps in this book will assist you to have a very different life. You have to be willing to step outside of yourself and to let go of your old patterns of thought. Invite curiosity and possibility into your life. Take time to go through all of the exercises placed in front of you. It is no accident that you have this book.

Take a few moments now and think about who else needs this book. Who will you give copies of this book to so they can create more love and compassion in their own lives? It might be someone you have just forgiven. It might be someone you suspect could be more patient, more loving, more understanding, more forgiving.

I believe that when we share and suspend judgment, we can truly help others. Everyone is walking around with old feelings of abuse, defeat, loss, fear, sadness, and who knows what else. Love them for who they are.

I truly do love you because I am you, and you are me, and we are both truly divine. Self-love and forgiveness have guided me. Being loving to others and forgiving of others and being kind, compassionate, supportive, and gentle with others will create an incredible sense of beauty and well-being in yourself.

This book will truly change your life story. You will find that forgiveness and love is the answer. I encourage you to share your perception with others and show others the radical transformation that is taking place within you. You may want to find some like-minded people who can support you on the journey.

It is a transformational time, and I am excited for you. You will notice the beauty and opportunities hidden beneath your own emotional scars. You will let go of past actions and perceived insults, disrespect, or grievances. You will release the energy tied up in old feelings against others or yourself and truly forgive. You will heal yourself — and others — inside and out.

My final words are: All you need is forgiveness and self-love. If you are willing, you now have the tools you need. You need only to have the heart to make the choice to release everyone and everything. You need only to open yourself up to expansion and allow in happiness and gratitude — and then watch your life change!

Join our community here for more support.

https://www.facebook.com/groups/
heartrepreneurswithterrilevine

Appendix

Colin Tipping, Radical Forgiveness
Worksheet *download the pdf* - https://
www.radicalforgiveness.com/pdf/
RFWorksheetMarch.pdf)

ACKNOWLEDGMENTS

I HAVE TO START BY THANKING my amazing husband, Mark. This book has taken me years to write, and he allowed me the space and freedom to write when I got the urge and understood the quiet time I needed alone to process and work through each chapter. I love you with all my heart.

I thank my niece Sarah Banfield with a gratitude beyond words. You read our story from my perspective. I am blessed and proud to be her aunt. She is a beautiful, mature, loving woman. Sarah taught me unconditional love. I love her even more than the very air I breathe itself.

I also thank Brian D. Ridgway. You met him in the book. I learned forgiveness with him and through him along with true self-love. No one has shown me more forgiveness, more unconditional love than Brian has.

I also thank my friends and client family members who encouraged me to write this book and to be transparent. They surrounded me with love and told me how important this book would be to their forgiveness process, and they encouraged me and inspired me to complete the book when I was stuck and unsure that I could share my entire life story.

I am blessed with the friends who stood in support of me through this journey, including Jay and Sheila Segal, Robin and Josh Schwartz, Sherri and Lisa Sacks-Epstein, Lisa Mondello, Elizabeth McNairney, Pete Winiarski, and my nephew Charles Boruchowitz.

I love, thank, and appreciate Radavie with all my heart and soul.

Frank Kresen, thank you for showing up to edit this book so brilliantly.

Finally, I send love and thanks for all the experiences, circumstances, and situations that have brought me to where I am today — even those who shut me out, like my sister Lynn. I also am grateful for my parents. They did the best they could with what they knew, and I believe they loved me deeply. I also continue to love them and miss them every day.

About the Author

Terri Levine is a business mentoring expert and the Chief Heart-repreneur® at www.Heartrepreneur. com. She is a best-selling author, keynote speaker, radio host (https://podcasts.apple.com/us/podcast/ heartrepreneur-radio/id1159942743), and TV host (www.Terri.TV) and appears regularly in the media as a business coaching and consulting expert.

Terri got fed up with how business was treating prospects, customers, employees, and vendors and decided to shift the business mindset. She and created the term "Heart-repreneur® to overhaul how we do business today. Dr. Levine is disrupting how business owners communicate, sell, and market their businesses with the Heart-repreneur® cause.

More than 4,000 people have embraced the Heart-repreneur® concept both online and offline with the formation of Heart-repreneur® Circles. (www.heartrepreneurcircles.com)

Her programs range from business coaching and business consulting, business-training seminars for business owners, business-coaching training programs to develop coaching skills, creating professional training courses for others in the field of business coaching, and providing additional products and services to companies seeking support to become Heart-repreneur®-based businesses. She provides free access to programs at https://www.heartrepreneuracademy.com and a free educational webinar at www.Heartrepreneur.com/freetraining.

CPSIA information can be obtained
at www.ICGtesting.com
Printed in the USA
FFHW011540111019
55480811-61279FF